Wings
OVER MONTANA

A CELEBRATION OF WILD BIRDS

FARCOUNTRY
PRESS

photography of **DONALD M. JONES** *introductory material by* **DANIEL CASEY**

To my soul mate, Tess.
Thank you for understanding and
sharing my obsession with birds.

—DONALD M. JONES

RIGHT: A male yellow-headed blackbird sings from atop a cattail. Its song sounds like a gate turning on rusty hinges.

FAR RIGHT: Showing off its seven-foot wingspan, a mature bald eagle takes flight.

TITLE PAGE: Four juvenile burrowing owls keep their eyes glued to a ferruginous hawk overhead.

FRONT COVER: A great gray owl glides silently over a mountain meadow near Yaak.

BACK COVER (TOP LEFT): This sandhill crane in central Montana is preparing to land.

BACK COVER (TOP RIGHT): A male mountain bluebird pauses before returning to its cavity nest near Gardiner.

BACK COVER (BOTTOM): Adopted as Montana's state bird in 1931, a western meadowlark perches itself high on the prairie grass near Havre.

COVER FLAP: Adorned in winter plumage, a white-tailed ptarmigan sits motionless in fresh snow in Glacier National Park.

ISBN 13: 978-1-56037-331-5
ISBN 10: 1-56037-331-8
Photographs © 2006 Donald M. Jones
© 2006 Farcountry Press
Photography and captions by Donald M. Jones
Foreword and chapter introductions by Daniel Casey

For more information about our books write Farcountry Press, P.O. Box 5630, Helena, MT 59604; call (800) 821-3874; or visit www.farcountrypress.com.

Created, produced, and designed in the United States.
Printed in Korea.

Table of Contents

With its winged meal firmly in its beak, a male mountain bluebird pauses on the top of a ponderosa pine.

Foreword

Daniel Casey
Northern Rockies Coordinator,
American Bird Conservancy

Sharp-tailed grouse dancing in the golden light of a prairie morning. An American dipper boldly disappearing underwater at the head of a torrent, only to bob up unscathed downstream with its stonefly prey. Wave after wave of migrant snow geese mirroring the rolling waves of grassland against the magnificent backdrop of the Rocky Mountain Front. These are but a few of the wonders awaiting the Montana birder.

Montana is a land of contrasts. The state has an elevational range of almost 11,000 feet from its lowest point in the Nashville warbler habitats along the Kootenai River to its highest point at Granite Peak in the Absaroka Range, home to gray-crowned rosy finches and white-tailed ptarmigans. Nearly 420 species of birds have been seen here, and more than 250 are known to breed, including 14 species of owls and 21 species of waterfowl. Montana is broad enough to include the western limits of several Great Plains species (including the Sprague's pipit and chestnut-collared longspur), while also capturing the easternmost population of some Pacific Northwest species (such as the chestnut-backed chickadee and Townsend's warbler). Boreal chickadees reach their southern limit in the mountains in and around Glacier National Park, while small populations of blue-gray gnatcatchers in the east and sage sparrows in the west represent the northernmost Rocky Mountain populations of these juniper- and sagebrush-nesting species.

Many bird species have their centers of abundance here. Sixty-five percent of the world's calliope hummingbirds breed in the Northern Rockies, as do half the world's Cassin's finches and American dippers. Three of the most sought-after birds in North America—the northern hawk owl, the great gray owl, and boreal owl—breed here, as does a significant proportion of the world's population of harlequin ducks, one of the continent's rarest sea duck species.

Montana also has an abundance of public lands and open spaces that offer opportunities for birding. Preserves such as Medicine Lake, Red Rock Lakes, Benton Lake, Bowdoin, and Ninepipe National Wildlife Refuges offer such spectacles as huge nesting colonies of American white pelicans and Franklin's gulls, water-dancing western grebes, and huge flocks of migrant shorebirds. Scenic backroads traverse native grasslands inhabited by longspurs, ferruginous hawks, lark buntings, and lark sparrows from the Crow Reservation in the southeast to Bureau of Land Management lands near Glasgow to the spectacular Rocky Mountain Front near Augusta. Montana's broad valleys and plains are drained by rivers whose names evoke the era of exploration and the lore of great fishing: the Madison, Missouri, Yellowstone, Bitterroot, Blackfoot, and Clark Fork. All offer up avian treats to the boater or roadside explorer: ospreys, yellow-breasted chats, lazuli buntings, Lewis's woodpeckers, spotted towhees, and spotted sandpipers.

But perhaps to many, the mountains are what most define Montana. It is here that the state's varied forests support ruffed, blue, and spruce grouse—and where the landscape so readily reveals the long-term effects of snow, ice, and fire. Each forest type has its distinctive bird community, from the red crossbills and pygmy nuthatches of the ponderosa pines to the pine and evening grosbeaks of the spruce-fir forests. High-elevation tundra inhabited by white-tailed ptarmigans is flanked by whitebark pine where Clark's nutcrackers and grizzly bears vie for pine nuts above the waterfalls where black swifts nest. State and federal forest lands, wilderness areas, and Glacier and Yellowstone National Parks offer the chance to enjoy these bird communities in a wide variety of settings.

Each season offers its rewards. January in Montana can be frigid, with strong winter winds and temperatures well below zero. Across the state, rough-legged hawks search the fields for their vole prey. In some years they share these open spaces with even rarer visitors from the north: the snowy owl and gyrfalcon. But the falcons may be more focused on gray partridges feeding in the open patches of wheat stubble between drifts.

Winter does not always yield easily to spring in Montana, but when it does, it is the birds that most loudly herald the change. Male red-winged blackbirds begin singing in the marshes, and flocks of swans, geese, and ducks start showing up

as soon as the first open water appears in March. By the first of April, hundreds of thousands of snow geese, tundra swans, and northern pintails wheel over Freezout Lake, while swallows course for emerging insects over Montana's rivers and lakes.

May is a month for travelers, as song-birds and shorebirds stop in Montana on their way to breeding grounds in Canada—a long way from their Mexican wintering areas. This is the time when many Montana birders might also travel, heading east to prairie oases such as Westby to see blackpolls and magnolia warblers, white-rumped sandpipers, and white-throated sparrows, spotted only infrequently elsewhere in the state.

But June is the time when Montana enjoys the most species, because all of the state's breeders have returned, and every habitat has its own mix of resident birds, each staking its claim through song and display. The short summers are a time for egg-laying and brood-rearing. Avocet chicks scurry through the saltgrass, house wrens busily fly to and from their nest holes with insects, and young burrowing owls line up for grasshoppers.

Fall migration starts early in Montana. Brilliant

rufous hummingbirds find July flowers to fuel up for the long flight to the tropics, and the shallow wetlands of summer begin to host mixed flocks of southward-bound shorebirds. By September, many of the breeding birds have left, the stunning western tanagers soon to be replaced by flocks of winter finches, such as common redpolls and snow buntings. Lines of tundra swans overhead in November and swarms of bohemian waxwings descend-ing on mountain ash berries remind us that the cycle continues.

Don Jones's photographs capture the essence of Montana's birds—the timeless cycles of migration, the remarkable diver-sity of species, the fascinating demonstra-tions of behavior. The images in *Wings Over Montana* draw us into reflection on the beauty of birds—and the wonders of nature. Enjoy.

The Steller's jay is one of two crested jays found in Montana; the other is the blue jay.

Grasslands

Daniel Casey

The largest number of North American grassland species is found in the northern Great Plains, including much of eastern Montana. Although many grassland species are on the decline, Montana is blessed with more native grassland habitat than any other western state (more than 12 million acres) and supports healthy populations of such species as the long-billed curlew, burrowing owl, lark bunting, and ferruginous hawk.

Though not outwardly as complex as forest habitats, grasslands vary in structure and species composition, resulting in distinct bird communities across the state. One suite of species depends mostly on very short grasslands, such as those found in prairie-dog towns and in heavily grazed areas (formerly by bison, now by cattle). Among these are the burrowing owl, which nests in prairie-dog and badger burrows, the McCown's longspur, and the mountain plover. In mixed-grass prairie areas with more bunchgrass cover, we find chestnut-collared longspurs, Sprague's pipits, and Baird's sparrows, along with upland sandpipers and sharp-tailed grouse. Montana is easily the best place to find these two suites in combina-

tion, with lots of public land on which to do so, widely distributed from Alzada to Big Timber, and from Plentywood to Browning. It's difficult to predict from year to year just where to find the right conditions to support a given species. Drought and grazing intensity can profoundly affect the condition of the prairie, and most grassland birds are at least partially nomadic to cope with this problem. Hence lark buntings might be common as far west as the foothills of the Rocky Mountain Front one year, and not found west of the Highwood Mountains the next.

Not all of the state's grassland birds are limited to the eastern prairies. Prairie falcons and golden eagles nest on cliffs throughout much of the state, including those western valleys with open grassland and sagebrush/grassland mosaics. Also in the northwest, remnant bunchgrass Palouse prairie supports long-billed curlews, short-eared owls, and grasshopper sparrows. Although many of these valley grasslands are seeing intense development pressure, there are many cooperative efforts to conserve and restore the largest blocks of native habitat— incorporating the habitat needs of birds into land management decisions and agricultural practices. Some species, such as the bobolink, are actually more common in irrigated hayfields than in native grassland habitat. Indeed, many of the birds that we think of as grassland species

also utilize Montana's agricultural habitats, from horned larks to introduced gamebirds such as the ring-necked pheasant and gray partridge.

Grasslands provide much more than nesting habitat to Montana's bird life. Seed crops, insects, and small mammals abound in these areas, attracting birds during all seasons. Many birds nesting in adjacent shrub and forest habitats rely heavily on grasslands for food, including eastern kingbirds, mourning doves, and loggerhead shrikes. Also Swainson's hawks and American kestrels, which are as prone to eating grasshoppers as they are to eating mice. Population explosions in grassland rodents, such as meadow voles, can support impressive numbers of hawks and owls during Montana winters. Rough-legged hawks can be found statewide most years, with hundreds of birds in areas such as the Mission Valley near Ronan. Snowy owls also appear during most winters, more often on the eastern prairies than in the western valleys, where some large concentrations of long-eared and short-eared owls overwinter in windrows. These owls join coyotes, magpies, and even great blue herons and gulls in feasting on voles during these peak years.

Montana's grasslands: surprising in their scope and diversity, and home to some of the state's most unique bird species.

The long-billed curlew, this one photographed near Malta, nests in Montana's shortgrass prairies. The long-billed is the state's largest sandpiper.

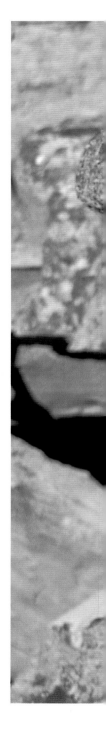

A juvenile short-eared owl in the Mission Valley takes time out for some morning calisthenics.

A female ferruginous hawk, Montana's largest buteo (genus of hawk with broad, rounded wings), watches over her young in a cliff nest near Cutbank. Found primarily on the prairie, these hawks nest in trees, on cliffs, or even on the ground.

FACING PAGE: A male (rooster) ring-necked pheasant at sunset. Although one of Montana's most recognized birds, the ring-necked pheasant is not a native but rather a Chinese import.

LEFT: The gray partridge, or Hungarian partridge, is an introduced Eurasian species that can be found on Montana's agricultural lands.

BELOW: A male sharp-tailed grouse races alongside his rival on a lek (mating ground) within C. M. Russell National Wildlife Refuge.

RIGHT: It's April and these sharp-tailed grouse near Great Falls take to the lek, which is a small piece of ground where the males defend tiny territories and perform their displays in order to attract females.

BELOW: Snowy owls generally are seen in Montana when winters to the north are harsh and food supplies are low.

RIGHT: A horned lark, the only species of lark native to the Western Hemisphere, sits atop sagebrush near Glasgow.

FACING PAGE: The chestnut-collared longspur is the smallest longspur in North America and is found in dense grass. This male was photographed near Malta while it searched the prairie floor for insects.

BELOW: A marbled godwit lands in a shortgrass prairie.

RIGHT: Brewer's sparrows are found in most of Montana's shrub grasslands. Their habitat is shrinking due to increased agriculture and housing developments. This male was found near the Big Hole River in the southwestern part of the state.

FAR RIGHT: High on most birders' lists is the Baird's sparrow. It is most easily found in the northeastern part of the state from Malta to Medicine Lake National Wildlife Refuge.

A marbled godwit chick lies motionless in the shortgrass prairie. As with all members of the sandpiper family, the young are out of the nest and foraging within hours of hatching.

A male common grackle calls from a caragana bush. Their thick bills
and keeled tails distinguish them from blackbirds.

FACING PAGE: A rough-legged hawk warms itself in the morning sun. Unlike the snowy owl, which migrates south into Montana only in harsh winters, this visitor from northern Canada and Alaska comes to the state every winter, usually arriving in late October and staying until April.

RIGHT: A male sage grouse flaunts his plumage in the morning's first light. Like the sharp-tailed grouse, the sage grouse uses the lek to attract a mate and sometimes dances throughout the night, particularly on moonlit nights—quite the romantic.

BELOW: The snow bunting is yet another visitor from the north. This bird can be found throughout Montana in the winter, with greater numbers being seen on the prairies in areas left vacant by migrating longspurs and sparrows.

LEFT: A Say's phoebe finds a perch from which to scan the surrounding ground for insects.

FACING PAGE: Young gray partridges huddle together on a shortgrass prairie. The gray partridge, or Hungarian partridge, produces some of the largest clutches of any bird, averaging fifteen to seventeen eggs—and sometimes as many as two dozen.

An upland sandpiper keeps a wary eye to the sky while perched upon a fencepost near Conrad. This sandpiper is considered threatened in much of its range.

A western kingbird hunts from a barbed-wire fence. The male performs a courtship ritual in which it flies up to fifty feet in the air and then tumbles down wildly.

RIGHT: Clay-colored sparrows frequent brushy areas away from trees. This bird defends its territory in a brushy draw near the Saskatchewan/Montana border.

FACING PAGE: A female eastern kingbird sits upon her nest tucked in a hawthorn tree. Look for kingbirds along Montana's rural roads hunting insects on the wing.

BELOW: The mountain plover is listed as a sensitive species in Montana. Look for this bird in shortgrass prairies, overgrazed pastures, and prairie-dog towns. The west end of C. M. Russell National Wildlife Refuge offers the best opportunity to view this bird.

LEFT: Though a songbird, this loggerhead shrike acts more like a raptor, hunting from a perch for game ranging from grasshoppers to birds its size.

FACING PAGE: This killdeer is no fool for laying her eggs in the open—once she leaves her nest, the eggs blend incredibly well with the surrounding rocks. Get too close and she performs a distraction display, such as dragging her wing as though it is broken.

After the breeding season, the bobolink (a member of the blackbird family) loses its black, white, and yellow plumage and looks more like the female, streaked and brown.

ABOVE: A male lark sparrow has made a meal of a katydid. The female lark sparrow is a ground nester with young fledglings after nine to twelve days. If disturbed by a predator or curious onlooker, fledglings can appear after only six days.

RIGHT: A male grasshopper sparrow sings in a Eureka meadow. These songbirds are usually heard rather than seen, as they are shy and tend to hug the cover of thick grasses.

Curious about what this golden eagle has in its talons, a coyote approaches. The eagle prefers to keep this small morsel of food to itself. The coyote retreats in haste, only to repeat its approach a few minutes later. This time, the coyote feels the effects of the eagle's talons, which send him wheeling down the mountain.

FACING PAGE: A short-eared owl in Ninepipe National Wildlife Refuge gives the camera a quizzical look. Look for these owls in the late afternoon and at dusk as they fly with slow, deep-winged beats over fields and marshes.

LEFT: In the Flathead Valley, a northern shrike hovers in search of prey. Northern shrikes come from northern Canada and Alaska to Montana during the late fall and winter, occupying those areas left vacant by the migrating loggerhead shrike.

BELOW: A male sage grouse takes flight from the lek. During the winter, sage grouse depend entirely on the soft evergreen leaves and shoots of the sagebrush for food.

Four burrowing owlets wait patiently for their parents to return with the entrée of the day: crickets. Owlets are known to virtually attack the adults when they arrive back at the nest, sometimes even knocking them over for the morsel. It's first come, first served in this family.

A savannah sparrow bursts into song at day's first light. One of North America's most well-distributed sparrows, they occur from Alaska to Baja California, from Florida to Hudson Bay.

South of Glasgow, a male McCown's longspur finds this lichen-covered boulder a good vantage point from which to survey his domain. Look for these longspurs in barren, open areas, such as overgrazed pastures.

ABOVE: A male lark bunting in breeding plumage strikes a pose near Harlem. Although called a bunting, the bird is a member of the family of New World sparrows.

RIGHT: An adult Swainson's hawk hunts from a roadside fencepost north of Great Falls. During migration, Swainson's hawks make some of the longest journeys of any hawk, traveling thousands of miles from the United States and Canada to Argentina.

ABOVE: Look closely and you will see why this eastern kingbird is a member of the flycatcher family.

FACING PAGE: A rock wren near Dillon fills a rocky draw with song. Rock wrens make their cup nests in fissures, tunnels, or cavities in rock.

RIGHT: An adult prairie falcon slices through the air north of Browning. While the peregrine falcon will take prey out of the sky, the prairie falcon typically captures its prey on open ground.

BELOW: A gyrfalcon braces itself against a strong wind near Freezout Lake Wildlife Management Area. A rarely seen winter visitor from the treeless Arctic, the gyrfalcon finds power poles a convenient and novel perch.

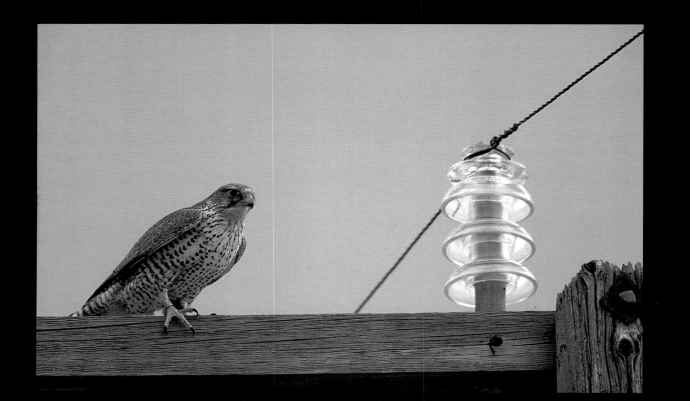

A male sage thrasher goes into full display atop a sagebrush near Bannack State Park.

A black-necked stilt wades through the shallows at Freezout Lake.
Adult male black-necked stilts tend to have a uniform black back,
while the backs of the females are brownish in color.

Wetlands

Daniel Casey

The wetlands in Montana include everything from the prairie potholes that speckle the northeastern grasslands and represent part of North America's "duck factory" to the broad shallow marshes such as Red Rock Lakes National Wildlife Refuge in southwestern Montana, where extensive bulrush stands support red-necked grebes, trumpeter swans, redheads, and black terns. Common loons reach their highest density in the western United States on the lakes of Montana's northwestern counties. Low-elevation lakes, marshes, and river oxbow complexes such as those in the Blackfoot, Big Hole, Madison, and Flathead Valleys are inhabited by American bitterns, wood ducks, Barrow's goldeneyes, and sandhill cranes.

Wetland habitats offer an abundance of food, unique nesting habitats, and resting areas for migrants. Some of Montana's best watchable wildlife opportunities are at wetland sites, where many species can be compared, studied, and enjoyed in open conditions on public lands. Birds and birders alike have benefited from the many wetlands protected and restored by fish and wildlife agencies. The hundreds of thousands of snow geese, tundra swans, and northern pintails at Freezout Lake Wildlife Management Area near Choteau, or the tens of thousands of mixed shorebirds at Bowdoin National Wildlife Refuge in spring and fall are also a testament to the productivity of large prairie lakes. Many smaller wetlands are ephemeral, present in spring just long enough for mallards and lesser scaups to form pair bonds and mate before selecting a prairie nest site. Montana's wet meadows—whether prairie swales, remote wilderness sedge bogs, or flood-irrigated hay meadows—offer up the ghostly winnowing of Wilson's snipes overhead and the loud bugling of sandhill cranes.

Look closer at a vibrant wetland during the nesting season, because many surprises await: a drake cinnamon teal stretching in the shallows; grebes and coots nesting on floating mats of vegetation barely above the surface; the precocial young shorebirds looking for food as soon as they hatch. In the denser cattails and sedges, gaudy yellow-headed blackbirds vie with (and usually out-compete) their smaller red-winged relatives for the best nesting territories over water. Common yellowthroats, marsh wrens, and both soras and Virginia rails are more often heard than seen in their marsh lairs. Much more visible are the trumpeter swans, nesting high on muskrat lodges. This species has been increasing in numbers away from its stronghold in the Centennial Valley, in part due to reintroduction efforts in the Flathead and Blackfoot Valleys. Common loons have also been benefiting recently from the hands of people, as "Loon Rangers" work with recreationists and homeowners to minimize disturbances at traditional nesting lakes during the nesting and brood-rearing seasons. Montana's loons winter primarily on the California coast, and hundreds of Canadian birds pass through Montana every fall, when large flocks can be seen at spots such as Ennis Lake.

This connection to birds that travel throughout the Western Hemisphere is perhaps no more dramatic than at Montana's wetland areas. The snow geese we see in spring have left California via southern Oregon, and some are headed all the way to Alaska's Wrangell Island to nest. Even more dramatic are the travels of such shorebirds as the American golden-plover, which nests in the high Arctic and passes through Montana on its way to wintering areas in southern South America. One can see twenty-two species of these long-distance migrant shorebirds in Montana in a typical year, in addition to the striking species (American avocet, black-necked stilt, willet, Wilson's phalarope) that call Montana home during the summer months.

Montana's wetlands: full of life, surprises, and spectacles.

FACING PAGE: Hundreds of red-winged blackbirds, as well as a handful of yellow-headed blackbirds, take flight over central Montana wetlands. There are an estimated 200 million red-winged blackbirds in North America.

LEFT: A male cinnamon teal stretches his wing, showing off the brilliant blue patch on his forewing. The cinnamon teal, the ruddy duck, and the whistling duck are the only waterfowl to nest in both North and South America.

BELOW: A male and female red-breasted merganser rest at Canyon Ferry Reservoir on their journey north. The red-breasted merganser is one of three species of mergansers found in Montana, the others being the hooded and the common. Both of these are far more common and will breed within the state.

LEFT: A pair of western grebes tends to their floating nest on Ninepipe Reservoir. Western grebes are much more numerous than the similar looking Clark's grebe, which differs in face pattern and bill color.

FACING PAGE: A juvenile osprey tests its wings high above Lake Koocanusa while its siblings await the arrival of their next meal. Ospreys have barbed pads on the soles of their feet to help grip the slippery fish that make up their diet.

ABOVE: An adult common loon sits motionless on its nest near Troy. The common loon produces from one to three eggs with both parents taking turns to incubate. Upon hatching, the young ride on their parents' backs for security until they are too big to do so.

FACING PAGE: A Virginia rail makes a brief appearance at the marsh's edge near the Bull River in western Montana. You are more likely to hear them than see them, so listen for what sounds like two rocks being struck together repeatedly: *wep wep wep wepwepwepppprrr.*

LEFT: A flotilla of American white pelicans makes its way across Freezout Lake on a foggy spring morning. These pelicans tried desperately to catch spawning carp in the shallows that morning. The fish seemed too big and slippery for the birds as, again and again, the birds tried to get fish into their mouths.

BELOW: A willet stretches its wings, showing its distinctive white wing stripe. When photographing along wetlands, the willet is one of the first birds to sound off if a predator, such as a northern harrier, comes into the area.

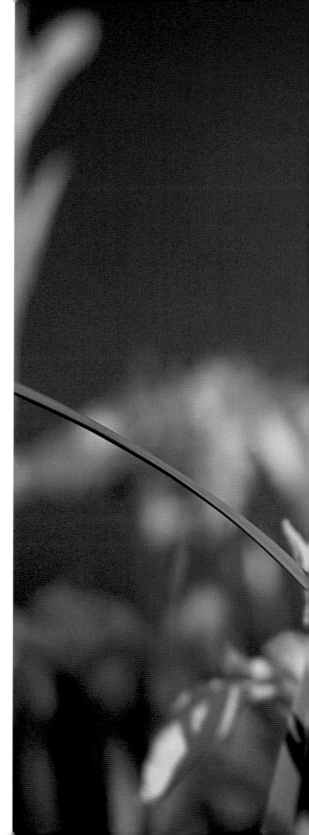

RIGHT: A male yellow-headed blackbird bursts out in song from an iris-laden cattail marsh in the Mission Valley. While some consider their song harsh, the bird deserves an "A" for style in its delivery.

BELOW: A common yellowthroat inches its way up a cattail to sing its musical tune, *wichety wichety wichety*. One of the more widespread wood warblers, the yellowthroat has up to fourteen subspecies.

LEFT: A male wood duck stretches its wings while swimming in a small lake near Yaak. In the small lakes that dot northwestern Montana, wood ducks compete with goldeneye ducks for cavity-nesting trees near the water.

BELOW: Its mouth full of waterborn insects, an American dipper pauses before flying up to its moss nest tucked under a bridge. The dipper has the distinction of being the only songbird that regularly swims.

ABOVE: Locked onto its target, a snow goose prepares for final approach. The snow and blue goose used to be considered separate species, but now the blue is considered a dark morph (darker color phase) of the snow goose.

RIGHT: On a cold March day along the Rocky Mountain Front, nine drake pintails and one hen fly low over the frozen marsh in a courtship flight.

LEFT: A red-necked grebe on a floating nest looks around nervously as a largemouth bass swims nearby. The nest not only serves as a place for egg incubation but also for copulation.

RIGHT: A sora near the Bull River of northwestern Montana works the marsh's edge in search of food. Within hours of hatching, sora chicks' eyes are open, they have downy feathers, and they are capable of independent movement—qualities that make them "precocial," or capable of a high level of activity from birth.

BELOW: A newborn Canada goose gosling slips out from under its mother to take a look at the world for the first time.

LEFT: A male marsh wren sings loud and often. In the West, marsh wrens are known to have as many as 150 songs in there repertoires.

FACING PAGE: Two American avocet parents escort their chick to safety. Later in life those long legs will be an asset, but for a chick they seem to be more of a burden.

BELOW: An American avocet sits motionless on a saline flat so as not to be detected. Avocet chicks, like sora chicks, are considered precocial.

A black-crowned night heron stands at the water's edge near a canal at Benton Lake National Wildlife Refuge. As its name suggests, this heron is nocturnal; but it will forage during the day. The night heron is notorious for feeding on chicks and eggs of rails and terns.

RIGHT: In search of food, a black tern hovers over a remote marsh along the Highline during a light summer rain. Black terns breed in marshes throughout most of the eastern two-thirds of Montana before heading south to wintering grounds in western South America.

BELOW: Swirling waters have not deterred this male harlequin duck from resting on a rock in McDonald Creek in Glacier National Park. After breeding, the male harlequin makes its way back to coastal waters, leaving the female to do all the incubating and chick-rearing.

65

RIGHT: A male lesser scaup keeps a watchful eye on his surroundings as he rests. Lesser scaups usually remain in the northern part of their range as long as there is open water and available food.

FACING PAGE: A flock of several hundred Ross's geese takes to the air from grain fields near Augusta. The shape of its bill is the best field mark to use to distinguish this bird from the snow goose. The Ross's bill is smaller and more stout than that of the snow goose.

A Forster's tern calls out from the shore of Freezout Lake. Unlike most terns, which capture prey by dipping or plunge-diving while in the air, Forster's also hunt from a perch.

RIGHT: A pair of Wilson's phalaropes take a break from spinning and strike an elegant pose. Phalaropes swim in tight circles while foraging. This spinning causes a small upwelling of water that transports prey, insects, and other small organisms to the surface.

BELOW: From a small pothole near Browning, a male redhead duck stretches in the morning light. Hybridization has occurred between redheads and canvasbacks, with males being most readily identifiable.

Near the base of the Mission Mountains, fourteen recently released trumpeter swans feed in the shallows of Ninepipe Reservoir.

If you could read this great blue heron's mind, you might see visions of sunny Florida. While most great blue herons migrate south, a number of them tough out the Montana winter. They hunt the waters that have not frozen, and also seek mice and voles.

A flock of tundra swans journeys north past Freezout Lake Wildlife Management Area, headed to their breeding grounds in northern Canada and Alaska. In March at Freezout Lake, the numbers of tundra swans can reach 10,000 as they rest and feed before continuing north.

FACING PAGE: A white-faced ibis takes flight along a canal in Benton Lake National Wildlife Refuge. Benton Lake has the highest concentration of nesting white-faced ibises in the state.

LEFT: A female northern harrier gently feeds one of her newborn chicks. The male northern harrier hunts and brings food back to the nest, exchanging it with the female while hovering in the air over the nest site.

BELOW: A spotted sandpiper nest lies hidden on the ground along the shore of Bull Lake near Troy.

A Franklin's gull feeds in the shallows of Freezout Lake. The Franklin's gull is the only gull that undergoes two complete molts each year.

Three male ring–necked ducks swim in the dark waters of a mountain lake in northwestern Montana. This duck is a powerful swimmer and can forage to depths of forty feet in search of a meal.

Snow geese land in the barley fields near Fairfield. Every year in late March, one of Montana's largest bird spectacles occurs: up to 500,000 snow geese converge on Freezout Lake Wildlife Management Area to feed and rest before their journey north to breeding grounds.

RIGHT: A lone kingfisher perches at sunset along the Bitterroot River near Missoula.

FACING PAGE: At dawn, a trio of sandhill cranes takes flight across the central prairies near Lewistown.

A great horned owl finds peace and quiet in a hardwood thicket within Pablo National Wildlife Refuge.

Woodlands

Daniel Casey

Montana's forests have been shaped into a multitude of variations by climate, elevation, fire activity, and the actions of people. Forest and woodland habitats often support the highest diversity of birds. Understory plants, trees of various ages, snags, downed logs, and fruit and seed crops each provide cover, nest sites, or food for one or more species. And in landscapes where the forest types themselves can vary from young, open stands to cathedral-like stands of old growth, bird life reflects that variation. Flammulated owls and Lewis's woodpeckers, for example, prefer open, mature stands of dry ponderosa pine forests, with large snags for nesting and patchy areas of grassland, shrubs, and seedling trees to produce their insect prey. Pygmy nuthatches and red crossbills prefer the canopy of these forests, where cone crops provide food. Denser stands of spruce, Douglas-fir, and grand fir are preferred by the Townsend's warbler, golden-crowned kinglet, and spruce grouse. Western tanagers and Swainson's thrushes offer a splash of color and a beautiful flute-like soundtrack, respectively, to many of Montana's mixed forests, from the larches and firs of middle elevations of the Kootenai National Forest to the more open pine, fir, and aspen stands of the Gallatin National Forest.

Montana has experienced extensive forest fires both historically and in recent years. While at first the results of such fires might seem to be devastating, many of the state's bird species are adapted to, and indeed prefer, the habitats created when forests burn. And some are the species that bring birders to Montana: black-backed and American three-toed woodpeckers, olive-sided flycatchers, and Townsend's solitaires are among the fire-dependent species that thrive during forest rejuvenation. The only known nesting area for northern hawk owls in the state is the extensive burned areas in Glacier National Park.

Ask people what their favorite tree in the western forest is, and quaking aspen is likely to be the answer. There is nothing quite like the shimmering chartreuse of new aspen leaves against a bright blue springtime sky, or those same leaves turned lemon yellow in the fall. But seek out aspens during the summer months as well, when mountain bluebirds and tree swallows add their own blue highlights to the landscape. Both nest in the cavities provided by red-naped sapsuckers and other woodpeckers that excavate in these trees. Across the more than one million acres of aspens in Montana, one can also find drumming ruffed grouse, and nesting warbling vireos, house wrens, veeries, and ovenbirds.

While aspens are often found in small groves within sagebrush areas and in conifer forests, they are also found in riparian (streamside) woodlands. These woodlands are where we find the greatest variety of birds. Indeed, estimates are that more than 70 percent of all Montana bird species use riparian areas during part of the year, even though these forests cover less than 2 percent of Montana's landscape. Gallery forests of black, narrowleaf, and plains cottonwood are the dominant riparian woodlands of the region. Eastern and western screech-owls, Vaux's swifts, wood ducks, and pileated woodpeckers are among the species that are highly reliant on mature cottonwood stands and the nesting cavities that they provide. Black-headed grosbeaks and orioles nest in the foliage of the canopy. Most of Montana's more than 300 pairs of bald eagles nest in this habitat. Streamside shrublands of willow, alder, redstem dogwood, and other broadleaf shrubs support their own suite of nesting species, including calliope and rufous hummingbirds, eastern kingbirds, yellow warblers, and cedar waxwings. Many of Montana's cities have parks with excellent examples of this habitat, including Greenough Park in Missoula, Riverfront and Two Moon Park in Billings, Giant Springs in Great Falls, and Lawrence Park in Kalispell. All the major rivers have public access sites that not only accommodate floaters, but often provide habitat to explore on foot.

Montana is indeed "Big Sky Country" and in many ways lives up to the boast of being "The Last Best Place." It is not merely glacier-capped peaks, nor slopes of pine and fir; not merely the river and mountain routes of famous explorers seeking the west coast, but also a vast, varied landscape of grass and lakes. It is a landscape complemented by rivers, bounded by mountains, and inhabited by fascinating and beautiful birds.

FACING PAGE: A yellow-rumped warbler feeds a much larger juvenile brown-headed cowbird on a backyard fence. Cowbirds are brood parasitic, meaning that they lay eggs in other birds' nests and leave the rearing of the young to the host species.

BELOW LEFT: As if flinging open a cape, a northern flicker opens out its wing to preen. There are two types of northern flicker: the "red-shafted" pictured here and the "yellow-shafted." These were once separate species that have been combined because of the extensive interbreeding that occurred in places where their ranges overlapped.

BELOW RIGHT: A house wren peers out of its nesting cavity. This species of wren is found so widely across North America that it has three distinct subspecies groups that some consider three separate species.

A common redpoll waits out a winter snowstorm on a prickly rosebush. During some winters in Montana, populations of the redpoll (a northern finch) can irrupt—or rapidly increase in numbers—and create large flocks of birds.

Winter wouldn't be complete without an opportunity to see bohemian waxwings strip the berries from mountain ash trees.

It's October at Logan Pass in Glacier National Park, and with it comes snow and a change of colors for the white-tailed ptarmigan: when the snow flies, the bird's color changes from summer brown to winter white.

RIGHT: A red crossbill perches on a lodgepole pinecone. The crossbill is the only bird in the world with a truly crossed bill, which allows it to bite and pry open conifer cones.

FAR RIGHT: Like bohemian waxwings, American robins eat ripe mountain ash berries.

ABOVE: A green-tailed towhee sings from the top of a fir tree near Dillon. When a predator endangers its nest, the green-tailed towhee lures it away by running on the ground with its tail in the air, mimicking a chipmunk.

RIGHT: This Clark's nutcracker soaks up the last rays of sun on a chilly 20-below-zero day. This bird was discovered by and named for Captain William Clark of the Lewis and Clark Corps of Discovery.

A cedar waxwing perches on a blossoming apple tree near Troy. Waxwings nest late in the season, when there are ample food sources, such as fruit, for their young.

Even the needles of this ponderosa pine dwarf the northern pygmy owl, the smallest owl in Montana. During the winter months, look for these owls hunting along roadsides, often perched on power lines.

RIGHT: An adult black-capped chickadee is poised at the entrance of its cavity nest. The black-capped chickadee is one of four chickadee species in Montana; the other three are boreal, chestnut-backed, and mountain chickadees.

BELOW: A Swainson's thrush searches the forest floor for unsuspecting insects. The Swainson's thrush is a long-distance migrant that winters in the Neotropics, the area comprising southern Mexico, Central and South America, and the West Indies.

ABOVE: One of Montana's favorite backyard birds, a male evening grosbeak perches on a Douglas-fir. The evening grosbeak has the largest bill in the North American finch family.

RIGHT: A golden-crowned kinglet aggressively raises its crown when another kinglet enters its territory. During very cold nights, kinglets survive by huddling together in protected areas such as dense conifer stands.

Looking as though it has a Fu Manchu mustache, this male white-crowned sparrow actually has a mouthful of insects.

LEFT: An adult sharp-shinned hawk waits near a bird feeder for another wave of common redpolls. Of the three accipiter species in Montana, the sharp-shinned hawk is the most adapted to urban areas.

RIGHT: The northern hawk owl was a rare winter visitor until 2005, when four pairs of owls took up residency in Glacier National Park.

BELOW: In search of insects, a gray-crowned rosy finch follows the receding snow line on Glacier National Park's Logan Pass.

A male ruffed grouse signals spring with a drum roll. The male grouse drums to lure females. When a female arrives, the male grouse fluffs up his neck feathers and fans out his tail in an elaborate "ruff."

RIGHT: At four and one-quarter inches, the pygmy nuthatch is Montana's smallest nuthatch. It feeds on the needles clustered at the tips of Douglas-fir and yellow pine branches.

BELOW: From a barren limb, a male rufous hummingbird guards his territory. Hummingbird feet are useful only for perching. Because of the structure of its feet and legs, a hummingbird has a difficult time walking, and sometimes something as simple as turning around on a perch forces the bird to hover.

ABOVE: The sunset-colored feathers on the head of an orange-crowned warbler are apparent if you look closely, but this bird is more easily recognized by its drab appearance and its song.

RIGHT: A male Tennessee warbler stands on a log near a watering hole in Westby. The Tennessee warbler (a member of the wood warblers) uses its sharp beak to probe flowers for insects and nectar.

Looking somewhat out of place with its bright plumage, the male western tanager takes refuge high in a Douglas-fir tree. During their short stay in Montana in the spring and summer, these Neotropical birds are favorites among fly fishermen, who watch them feed on flying insects along the shoreline.

An adult male black-headed grosbeak is poised near Fort Peck Reservoir. It takes two years for male black-headed grosbeaks to develop their full adult plumage; subadult males are more mottled in color. Although one-year-olds are able to breed, most females prefer older, more brightly-colored males.

In a small pool of water in Westby, a male Baltimore oriole takes a spring bath. This oriole is another Neotropical migrant that flies north to Montana in the summers to breed.

FACING PAGE: The largest owl in North America, this great gray owl is tucked in an aspen grove along the Bitterroot River near Missoula. Some great grays are migrants from the north and some are year-round residents of western Montana.

BELOW LEFT: A dark-eyed junco searches for food among the fallen logs on a cold February day. There are four recognized populations of dark-eyed juncos; the bird pictured here is an "Oregon" junco.

BELOW RIGHT: A Canada jay or gray jay makes good use of a willow branch. Known also as camp robbers or whiskey-jacks, gray jays become very acclimated to people and are common visitors to campsites, bird feeders, and dog-food bowls.

RIGHT: The northern saw-whet owl is strictly a nocturnal owl that finds daytime refuge in dense stands of cover, sometimes only a few feet off the ground. When encountered during the day, these owls are often easy to approach.

FACING PAGE: A female calliope hummingbird incubates her eggs in this lichen-covered nest.

A pileated woodpecker looks out of place in this small tree. At seventeen inches, the pileated is Montana's largest woodpecker, and the second largest in North America.

An adult red-tailed hawk in flight displays its namesake tail feathers against a royal blue sky. Montana's most common hawk, its plumage can vary in color from the white of a "Krider's" red-tailed hawk to the black of a "Harlan's" red-tailed hawk.

This blue grouse is in the act of displaying in order to attract a mate. An inhabitant of high-elevation, conifer forests, the blue grouse is not as tame as the spruce grouse, but the blue is generally easy to approach, particularly when it is displaying.

LEFT: A chestnut-backed chickadee perches at the entrance of its cavity nest. This bird is best found in the northwestern portion of Montana.

RIGHT: A male Townsend's warbler sings from its flowery perch in northwestern Montana's Purcell Mountains. The Townsend's warbler is the western counterpart of the black-throated green warbler that lives in eastern deciduous forests.

BELOW: A yellow warbler, sensing its vulnerability, takes a hurried bath in a small watering hole.

RIGHT: An eastern blue jay surveys the bird feeder below. Over the last ten to fifteen years, the blue jay has become a more common sight at Montana bird feeders.

FAR RIGHT: An electric blue male lazuli bunting bursts out in song along Pauline Creek in western Montana's Mission Valley. Lazuli buntings do not learn their songs in the nest, instead one-year-old males return to the breeding grounds and learn the songs from older males, a process known as "song-matching."

Half way up a spruce tree, a male spruce grouse is in display along Glacier National Park's North Fork Road. Known also as a "fool's hen," the spruce grouse is easily approached, but difficult to find.

ABOVE: A male blackpoll warbler rests on a lichen-covered rock in Westby. A summer resident of Canada's boreal forests, the blackpoll visits Montana only when it is migrating in late May and again in late August or early September.

RIGHT: Although it is generally secretive, the male spotted towhee climbs on tall, visible perches when it is establishing its breeding territory.

FACING PAGE: A male Wilson's warbler takes a break from feeding along a mountain road to look at the camera. Wilson warblers are noted for their ability to catch flies in the air.

RIGHT: A male Nashville warbler pauses along a logging road near Libby. The Nashville warbler has a complete eye ring, unlike the broken eye ring of its territorial cousin, the MacGillivray's warbler.

BELOW: An American pipit hunts grasshoppers among the alpine wildflowers of Logan Pass in Glacier National Park.

LEFT: A mountain chickadee, with its distinctive black mask, is a regular winter visitor to most western Montana bird feeders.

FACING PAGE: A canyon wren sings a song that echoes off the nearby rock cliffs. With its overgrown feet, flat head, and long bill, the canyon wren can get into the narrowest of crevices in vertical rock cliffs where it forages.

FACING PAGE: A juvenile varied thrush perches during an April snowfall. Although it can be found in the pine forests of western Montana, a varied thrush is more often heard than seen—listen for its single long whistle that sounds like a trill or a buzz.

BELOW LEFT: A resident of pine forests, the male black-backed three-toed woodpecker tends to its cavity nest. This bird and its cousin, the northern three-toed woodpecker, thrive in the areas scorched by wildfire in western Montana.

BELOW RIGHT: Common feeder birds in Montana, pine siskins often do not exhibit any fear when approached.

The small, drab
Empidonax com-
plex of flycatchers
are difficult to tell
apart, but you can
differentiate these
birds by voice,
habitat, and their
manner of nesting.
This willow fly-
catcher can be dis-
tinguished from its
cousin, the alder
flycatcher, by its
song.

Found in mountain pine forests during breeding season, Townsend's solitaires move to lower elevations in winter and gather in groups to feed on juniper berries. John J. Audubon named this bird in 1838 after a young ornithologist named John K. Townsend.

Because they are noctural and live at elevations over 5,000 feet, boreal owls are one of the most difficult birds to find in Montana, next to the flammulated owl.

RIGHT: Two long-eared owl chicks peer out from their nest in the Flathead Valley. Long-eared owls often nest in discarded magpie nests.

BELOW: A male Bullock's oriole blazes orange against the white blossoms of a serviceberry tree. Bullock's orioles are found in western Montana, while the Baltimore orioles inhabit the eastern portion of the state. Where the ranges overlap, hybridization may occur.

FAR RIGHT: A spotted towhee perches in the thorny jungle of a wild rose bush.

BELOW LEFT: A male Williamson's sapsucker takes a break from excavating a new cavity nest. Usually male and female woodpeckers look alike, but the male Williamson's sapsucker looks so different from the female (which has a brown head, barred back, and black breast) that they were once thought to be two distinct species.

BELOW RIGHT: The brown thrasher is a secretive bird that inhabits the briar patches and thickets of eastern Montana. The thrasher can sometimes be heard using its beak to scrape away leaves, searching for insects.

The cone of a white-barked pine dwarfs this red-breasted nuthatch. The bird prefers conifer seeds to insects, and when seed crops fail, the bird moves south.

ABOVE: Named after the explorer Meriwether Lewis, the Lewis's woodpecker not only feeds on insects in the same manner as other woodpeckers (excavating insects from under the bark or surface of trees), but it also catches insects on the wing like a flycatcher.

RIGHT: A female pine grosbeak feeds on snowberries along the Kootenai River near Troy. Like rosy finches, the pine grosbeak has throat pouches for carrying food.

Tundra swans wing their way north along the jagged
Rocky Mountain Front near Choteau.